STRESS?
NOT FOR ME!

Dr. Rosemary Maturure (Africa University, Librabry Dept, Zimbabwe)

Mr. Leslie Chiuswa (Africa University, Student Affairs, Zimbabwe)

Dr. Priscillah Muchemwa - Munasirei (Africa University, College of Social Sciences, Theology, Humanities & Education, Zimbabwe)

Chances Inc
Embrace Yourself

Stress! Not For Me!

First Edition 2024 (Paperback)
By Rosemary Maturure, Leslie Chiuswa and Priscillah
Muchemwa - Munasirei
Copyright © 2024 Rosemary Maturure, Leslie Chiuswa and
Priscillah Muchemwa - Munasirei

First Published in Harare, Zimbabwe by Chances Inc
ISBN: 978-1-77933-707-8

Edited By: Audrey Chirenje

Typesetting: Chances Inc

Printed By: Media Essentials

Cover Design By: Haniel Creates

DISCLAIMER

This is a non-fiction book. Any names, characters and incidents portrayed in it are used to inspire, motivate and for emphasis and are told from the Author's perspective.

Dedication

We dedicate this book to all the people who are suffering from stress and to our family members who supported us in writing this book.

Contents

Acknowledgments

As the authors we would like to express our gratitude to all those who made contributions to the putting up of this book on Stress Management. The journey in the success of this project was a collective effort and we appreciate all the support, guidance, and encouragement that we received as we were coming up with this book.

We express our earnest appreciation to our families and loved ones. Your firm support, understanding, and patience throughout the journey were invaluable.

We would like to thank our editor, Audrey Chirenje who skillfully polished and shaped this book. Your commitment to high quality and deep insights has greatly strengthened the quality of the final product. We are indebted for your contributions.

We extend our gratitude to the publishing team. Your professionalism, guidance, and expertise have been instrumental in transforming our manuscript into a published work. We appreciate your dedication to bringing this book to life and making it accessible to a wider audience.

To our readers, thank you for choosing this book and for your commitment to finding ways to manage and overcome stress in your lives. We hope that the strategies and insights shared in this book will make a positive impact on people's well-being, mental health and stress management.

With deepest appreciation,

Dr. Rosemary Maturure

Mr. Leslie Chiuswa

Dr. Priscillah Muchemwa - Munasirei

Preface

Stress has affected many people and some people end up losing their minds because of stress. We are thrilled to share with you the knowledge, insights, personal experiences, and professional expertise in the field of stress management.

Stress has become an ever-present companion in our lives as individuals, families and organisations. Stress affects individuals from all walks of life, impacting on emotional well-being and physical health, relationships. The Authors sincerely believe that understanding stress is crucial for one to lead a balanced and fulfilling life.

The purpose of this book is to offer readers a thorough guide to stress, its causes, and its effects on the mind and body. This book provides information on personal experiences working with individuals facing various stressors, practical tools and strategies to effectively manage stress at home, in a family and in the communities.

This book provides a wealth of information on the following:

- Causes of stress
- Effects of stress
- Symptoms of stress
- Framework/Theoretical Framework on Stress Management
- The role of Professional Counsellors in stress management
- How stress affects students and staff in institutions of higher learning
- Suggestions/ Solutions to stress management

The intention of writing this book is to give valuable insights, practical strategies supporting individuals and community to manage stress and improve well-being.

It is important to note that stress management is a lifelong journey.

We sincerely hope that this book serves as a guide, a source of inspiration, and a companion on your journey towards stress management and well-being. As you delve into these pages, we encourage you to approach the content with an open mind, engage in self-reflection, and embrace the strategies that resonate with you.

We would like to express our deepest gratitude to our families and loved ones who provided unwavering support, those in the academic field and many more.

With warmest wishes,

Dr. Rosemary Maturure

Mr. Leslie Chiuswa

Dr. Priscillah Muchemwa - Munasirei

About The Authors

DR. ROSEMARY MATURURE

Dr. Rosemary Maturure is a University Librarian at Africa University in Mutare, Zimbabwe. She has worked in School libraries and academic libraries since 1996. She has been a University Librarian since 2007. She holds a PhD in Library and Information Studies from the University of Botswana, Master's Degree and Bachelor's Degree in Library and Information Science from National University of Science and Technology, Zimbabwe. She is a seasoned librarian with 25 years of experience. She is reliable, honesty, hardworking forward-thinking library administrator, possesses a strong understanding of library management and day today running of the library. She has been involved in research activities which assist her to develop various techniques for best explaining and instilling research skills in students. She is currently a member of Zimbabwe Universities Library Consortium (ZULC) and is the Chairperson of that Consortium (2021 - 2024). She is the Electronic Information for Libraries (EIFL) Copyright Coordinator in Zimbabwe since 2021.

MR. LESLIE CHIUSWA

Mr. Leslie Chiuswa is a Registered Counsellor currently working as University Counsellor and Head of the Counselling and Career Services Unit at Africa University in Mutare, Zimbabwe. He is a seasoned Mental Health and Student Affairs Practitioner who has been working in the Higher Education fraternity since 2009. He has held various positions in University setting; Administration Officer, Acting Manager, Regional Student Advisor, Student Affairs Department. He holds a Master of Science in Counselling, a Bachelor of Science in Counselling all from the Zimbabwe Open University and is currently pursuing a Ph.D. in Consulting Psychology with the University of South Africa. Mr. Chiuswa is registered with the Allied Health Practitioners Council of Zimbabwe (AHPCZ), a member of the Zimbabwe Association for Family Therapists and Professional Counsellors (ZAFTPC) and Ministry of Health and Child Care Psycho-social team member. He is actuated by the core values of professionalism, ethical consciousness, integrity and diligence.

DR. PRISCILLAH MUCHEMWA - MUNASIREI

Dr. Priscillah Muchemwa - Munasirei is a Lecturer of Sociology and Child Rights at Africa University. She has extensive experience of working in higher education institution. Dr Munasirei has 15 years' experience working at Africa University, with six years of these spent working in the administration and the other nine in the academic field. She holds a PhD and Masters in Rural Development from the University of Venda in the Republic of South Africa, a Post-graduate Diploma in Social Work from Women's University in Zimbabwe, a Bachelor of Social Sciences in Sociology from Africa University, a Diploma in Education from the University of Zimbabwe, and a certificate in Family and Health Studies from Mutare Teacher's College. She currently serve as the as the Head of Department in the Social Sciences and also teaches and supervise honors, Masters and PhD research projects. She coordinates the graduate Masters and DPhil programmes in Child Rights and Childhood Studies. Her research interests are in issues related to sexual reproductive health, gender, livelihoods, food security, child protection and participation, women, water and community participation.

INTRODUCTION

In the fast-paced and demanding world we inhabit, stress has become an ever-present force that impacts our lives in profound ways. From the pressures of academic achievement to the challenges of juggling personal and professional responsibilities, the weight of stress can be overwhelming.

Welcome to this stress management textbook, a comprehensive guide designed to equip you with the knowledge, skills, and strategies needed to navigate the intricate path towards stress resilience. As you embark on this journey, we invite you to suspend your preconceived notions about stress and open your mind to a new perspective—one that views stress not as an insurmountable obstacle, but as a catalyst for personal transformation.

In the pages that follow, we will delve deep into the nature of stress, exploring its physiological, psychological, and emotional dimensions. We will unravel the intricate web of stressors that pervade our lives, be they environmental, social, or internal.

As you navigate through each chapter, remember that the path to stress resilience is not linear. It is a process of self-discovery, growth, and adaptation. It requires patience, self-compassion, and an unwavering commitment to your well-being. You are not alone on this journey-within these pages; you will find the guidance, support, and resources to help you navigate the challenges that lie ahead.

How will suffering end? How can people be helped to reduce stress in their lives? Why are people's lives messed up? Why is there suffering in the world?

Everyone experiences mental health and that has to be addressed as noted by the World Health Organisations (WHO 2023) who said everyone experiences stress to some degree and the way we respond to stress, however, makes a big difference to our overall well-being.

We all go through stress in our lives because of the different circumstances that we face as individuals, families or groups. No matter how this affects us we need to be careful on how to manage it, this can be through family members, friends or counsellors.

Stress can end up affecting our health and the way we relate with others/ affects us physically, emotionally and mentally. This book will help us understand how to handle issues when they come our way.

We have seen students, faculty and staff members stressed for the time that we have worked at institutions of higher learning and we wondered what could be done to solve this.

Institutions of higher learning have come up with departments of counselling due to the great demand from the learners and employees. This has seen experts in the profession of counselling being hired to provide services. This book was written by experts to provide information and guidance on how stress can be reduced.

CHAPTER 1

Overview Of Stress

What Is Stress?

Seeing people suffer in families, workplace, in the country and worldwide is painful. Being part of an academic institution, observing from the communities where they stay, the Authors decided to come up with this book to help people cope with stress. This was probably because they did not know what to do or how to come to terms with the problems. These challenges emanated from homes, friends, communities, workplaces and from employers. There are many issues that can cause stress and these include health, financial challenges, poor planning, failure to adjust after losing a loved one etc. Corsica and Bradley (2018) observed the same and noted that potential sources of stress range from major life events such as death of a loved one, divorce, or job loss to "daily hassles" such as traffic and interpersonal annoyances.

Demand for counselling is increasing everyday as people face pressure in families, communities, and organisations. Provision of such services does not match the demand as people continue to suffer in their places.

People get stress from pressure of work, failing to take losses and so forth. Families are encouraged to adapt to their life style, help each other, go for counselling, and seek help from friends and relatives.

Stress is defined by Pastorino and Doyle-Portillo (2012) as any event or environmental stimulus (stressor) that one respond to because he/she perceive it as challenging or threatening.

The pressures or demands placed upon an organism to adjust or adapt to its environment, Nevid (2012). Stress is the inability that individuals undergo to try and accept changes that take place in one's life. Stress does come and go and it comes from internal or external experience in life.

Stress is not a disease but it can lead to physical or mental condition and death if it is not addressed well. People must be well informed on how to deal with it to avoid these mental challenges. This can be avoided by reading materials that is shared by experts in the area of counselling, one can also go for counselling services. Stress leads to poor performance at work, low productivity at home, and discord in the family. Family members need to support one another and they need positive minds to tackle the stress challenges.

Organizations have to work together with counsellors to make sure that this issue is addressed properly and that welfare for the employees is addressed. Any environmental or life event perceived by the individual as threatening to his or her physical or psychological well-being and exceeding his or her capacities to cope causes bodily or mental tension and may be a factor in disease causation (Gebhart and Schmidt 2013).

Ways of dealing with stress

Human beings need each other in life, it is therefore crucial that we help each other in life. People are stressed after they lose their jobs, losing a loved one, poor working conditions at the work place, abuse, failures to achieve one's goals etc. There are many ways that people can help each other to deal with stress in families and at work places. People need to treat each other with love and respect, evaluate our living styles, focus on oneself, seek counselling, and create a conducive environment. These ways will make life bearable, comfortable and enjoyable. It is my responsibility, your responsibility and our responsibility to help each other.

Showing love and respect

Love covers it all and is very important in one's life, it is important that this is showed so that one will be free to share what will be in the heart and also to have trust in each other. In a family and at an institution if people love each other and show respect it will be easy to seek help from each other and sharing of inner thoughts.

Evaluation of living styles

It is good to be real life models for the family as parents. Children live what they see and observe in the family setup. As parents we need to make sure that when our children look at us they admire us, we need to practice healthy living styles and afford stresses. We need to make sure that life is good and enjoyable for all people in our households. If we fail to deal with stress in our homes it may affect children as well. It is good to avoid abuse of alcohol and drugs.

Focus on yourself

One has to eat healthy and good food so that the body can look good and adapt to body challenges. It is good that one watches over his/her body weight and exercises to maintain a good structure. If one neglects himself/herself it becomes a problem which can end up affecting mental health. One needs not to be isolated but be with friends, relatives and colleagues. One needs to have enough sleep, take rest and interact with others.

Talk about it

Have regular talks as a family as this can help one to open up. Failure to talk as a family leads to suicide if one is not helped or thinks that no one is there for him or her. Talk to someone that you trust and get help. In families this can be noticed when a member of the family is quiet and looks worried most of the time. In organizations when one is stressed work does not go on well and production will be lowered. It is therefore important that organization have regular training and help their employees on how to overcome stress to improve productivity.

Create a health environment

It is good to have a welcoming home and good work environment that is good for all members to reduce stress. Family members are supposed to participate and make sure that the environment is conducive for habitation.

Get professional help.

Professional help is very important in helping someone who is stressed. When one struggles with healthy issues or feels overwhelmed by stress, it is good to seek help from a professional counsellor. A counsellor is licensed and trained to help people cope with pressure from home or work. Some institutions realized the importance of a counsellor and they hire one to assist in offering these services. They come up with strategies to manage stress effectively and make behavioral changes to help improve one's health.

CHAPTER 2

Causes Of Stress

Introduction

Dealing with and managing stress is very important as it plays a crucial role in our overall general and mental health and well-being. However, dealing with stress is related to and depends upon our awareness of and knowledge about what causes the stress in the first place. Knowing the source of stress leverages a person to take the necessary steps to try and deal with and reduce the effects of stress. Also acknowledging that stress is as common as colds and a normal reaction to the external and internal dynamics is also important. Stress has many, varied and complex causes and this makes identification and pinpointing exact causes a daunting task. Work pressure, academic pressure, marital conflicts and many others haunt the young and old alike. This chapter is dedicated to looking at the causes and effects of stress. Effects of stress to the individual mainly the physical, psycho-emotional, behavioral and social effects shall also be tackled.

Causes of stress

Stress has many and varied causes across different personalities and individuals. What may be regarded as simple and mundane by one person can be treated as a serious stressor by another individual. Driving in a heavily congested city can be a source of stress for somebody whereas someone else can take advantage of the situation to listen to good music or a favorite preacher. Stress is normally triggered by events which are happening in our lives and we feel the resources that we have are inadequate to deal with the pressures we are experiencing. There are basically two sources of stress namely; internal and external (Melgosa, 2008). These shall be looked at in greater detail below. Causes of stress are organized into the following categories; personal, family and friends, employment and study, housing issues and money challenges. However, the conceptual frameworks for causes of stress shall take precedence.

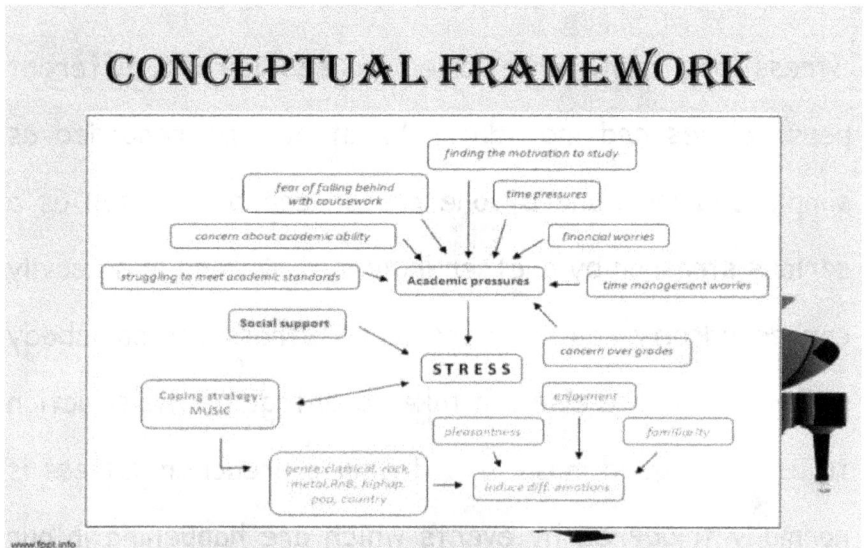

Fig 2.1: Conceptual framework for student stress

Job stressors

Job related factors:
- Job identity
- Job demands
- Work load
- Responsibly
- Role ambiguity
- Role conflict

Organisational factors:
- Organisational structure
- Policies and procedures
- Pay & benefit
- Recognition & promotion
- Job security
- Leadership style
- Training programmes
- Organisational justice
- Shift work

Interpersonal relations factors:
- Peer support
- Manager support
- Customer behaviours
- Communication quality

Working environment factors:
- Working conditions
- Facilities
- Space for work
- Heath/cold
-

Individual factors:
- Gender
- Age
- Marital status
- Education
- Personality
- Intelligence
- Coping style
- Financial status
- Dependent children

Socio- cultural factors:
- Attitudes
- Values
- Believes
- Family support
- Religious believes

Physical health:
- Fatigue
- Disordered eating
- Cardiovascular diseases
- Musculoskeletal disorders

Mental health:
- Sleep disturbance
- Lack of concentration
- emotional exhaustion
- Depression
- Anxiety
- Intolerance

Social health:
- Interpersonal conflict

Employee impact

Quality of work life

↓

Job satisfaction

↓

Organisational commitment

Employee outcome

Motivation

↓

Turnover

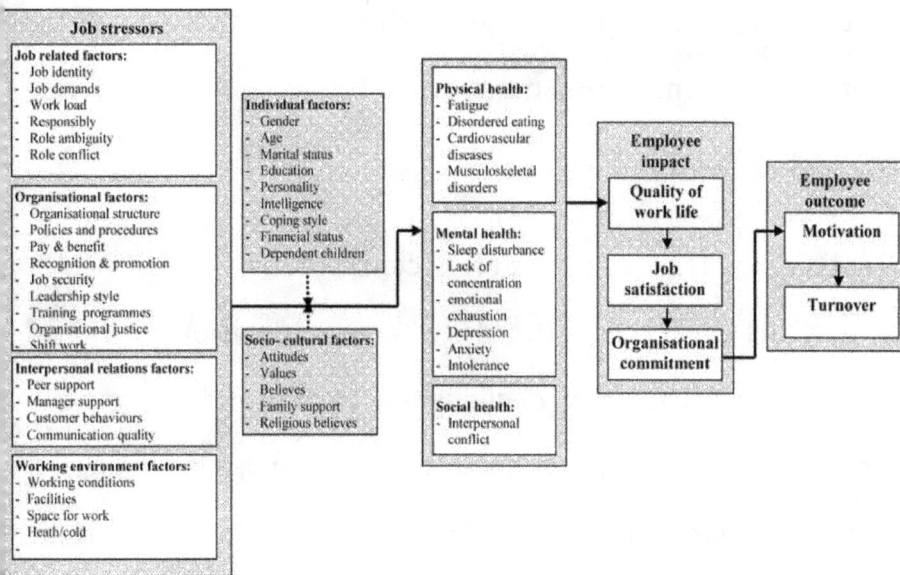

Fig 2.2: Conceptual framework for job stress

Personal causes of stress

At a personal level, there are several issues affecting an individual which can inevitably lead to stress. These include but not limited to; conflicting choices, illness or injury, pregnancy and becoming a parent, long-term health problems, organizing a complex event, transition to adulthood, transition to university, uncertainty, events outside our control and personality type.

Facing conflicting choices or dilemmas

Navigating life, we are often confronted with difficult situations and conditions wherein decision making becomes difficult and challenging. In the end a decision and course of action is supposed to be pursued despite our indecision. This puts a lot of pressure on us and this becomes overwhelming. Every course of action we may deem appropriate may have its own ramifications, often unwanted and negative and mostly we are not comfortable with it. What shall I do? What is the impact of choosing A over B? We are faced with a barrage of questions demanding answers. Ethical dilemmas have long been touted as sources of stress. A female student who seeks to accomplish academic excellence faces challenges and may not perform to expectations. The Lecturer demands that for the student to pass she should give into sexual demands. This presents a moral and ethical dilemma. What shall I do? Can I give in? What if we are caught? What will my parents and peers say? In the work setting, ethical issues are also common and navigating the difficult issues which arise can be daunting. In a study, Menzel (1996) posited that ethics stress was the leading cause of work pressure in government employees.

Illness or injury

There is an inextricable link between mental health and physical health. One cannot exist apart from the other. That is what the World Health Organization defines health as the state of "physical and mental well-being not just the absence of disease (WHO)". Therefore, stress is inevitable when we face an illness or injury because our minds ponder about the reality of the pain we are experiencing and also the prospects or outlook concerning the disease. Stress related to or linked with illness or injury can linger for as long as the condition is still there. This is often exacerbated by lack of social support from significant others. During the COVID-19 pandemic for example, there were many people who were stressed because covid-19 was lethal. Covid-19 evoked stress related to existential concerns and questions such as; am I going to die and leave my family? What will happen to my children? Is my spouse going to remarry? Are some of the questions which many had to deal with. This caused stress and anxiety and often made symptoms worse. Researchers in the area of covid-19 coined a term to describe those who experienced covid-19 for longer periods of time which was covid-19 long haul. Long haul patients experienced chronic stress leading to other physical conditions or psycho-somatic ailments as shall be described under the effects of stress section.

Pregnancy and becoming a parent

It can be exciting to anticipate the arrival of a new member of a family. The prospects of adding to the family a new life, a bundle of joy is fulfilling and gratifying to many people. Nevertheless, stress can also be linked to this predominantly positive development. Situations which cause stress include an unwanted pregnancy by a teenager attending school. The pregnancy under this situation can cause a lot of forebodings of fear and anxiety as parents and in-laws may not approve of the union. Both or one party may be too young to be a parent but the reality will be that new life is coming! Stress under these circumstances can be multi-pronged. All the parties to the issue can be stressed, the one carrying the pregnancy, the boy or man and the parents. Permanent marks have often been made especially to the young lady as a lot of harsh words are often spoken which many forget but only the young lady! In addition, even married couples experience stress when resources to support the new family member are inadequate. With the harsh economic environment, workplace compulsory redundancies due to the covid-19 pandemic, a new family member may put additional strain on an already stressed couple.

Long-term or terminal health problems

Suffering for a short period of time can be unsettling. Suffering for long periods of time due to chronic conditions can be mentally, physically and emotionally disconcerting. All of us strive to be and prefer being healthy and well. When chronic sicknesses come, issues of denial and anger are not uncommon. Stress comes and the longer the health condition lasts the more chronic the stress gets culminating in depression. Many people who suffer from chronic conditions such as; HIV/Aids, cancer, diabetes mellitus, heart problems among others require support and assurances of love in order to minimize stress. Suppose one is taking medication for chronic conditions and is constantly reminded that their lifestyle led to the disease, this definitely leads to stress! A person on HIV/Aids medication can be labeled loose or have low morals and this does not augur well with mental health which often deteriorates. Chronic health challenges require constant counselling care and support to deal with stress and various other issues related to coping and existential realities. There are times when the illnesses get terminal and counselling is required to face the reality and inevitability of death.

Organizing a complex event

This can be at school, work or church. You may be a holder of a position or requested to be part of a committee with specific and time limited frames of references. A big event on the calendar has been put in your hands to do the planning process. All eyes are on you and deadlines are beckoning! This can cause stress for the duration of the process. In Universities, planning of events such as; graduation, board meetings, matriculation are often demanding and often lead to stress. Generally, planning weddings, get together programmes, church annual major gatherings among others can also lead to stress. In all these events, individuals might break down and fail to cope. Committees usually make life easier and devolve responsibilities.

Transition to adulthood

The development of a human being progresses from birth to death. At each stage there are critical and inevitable milestones some which can cause stress. The adolescence period in particular has been shown to be characterized by storm and stress (Hall, 1983). It is a transitional period between childhood and adulthood. Significant physical, emotional, mental and social upheavals are taking place and the adolescent is often ill-prepared to face the storm due to inadequate experience. To exacerbate the situation, the brain itself would not have developed adequately to deal with difficult situations (Brown, 2002). The physical changes which occur in both boys and girls, for example; development of pubic hair, onset of menstruation, changes in voice, hormonal fluctuations, pimples and many others can cause stress due to their novelty. In addition, many confrontations and squabbles with parents occur during this stage. On the other hand, adolescents want "freedom" while on the other; parents consider the youth to be ill-prepared and too inexperienced to excurse on unchartered waters. Youths want to be treated as adults but the adults due to experience often anticipate pitfalls which the youth could be oblivious of. All these if not handled circumspectly, can lead to stress by both the parents and the youth.

Adulthood has its unique share of responsibilities and obligations. When a youth completes college, society, family and even the young adult him or she expect to be independent and chart on a path. However, lack of financial stability and the death of employment opportunities often lead to stress. Young adults often compare with their peers who have been fortunate enough to secure formal jobs. Comparing often leads to even more and heightened stress.

Uncertainty and stress

There are many situations and conditions which can cause stress in life. We are also different as we are many hence the way we perceive situations differ from person to person. Uncertainty about the future and the attendant negativity often hinders our coping when events happen as our outlook is already grim (Thomas, 2019). When we are negative, we may not take the necessary steps to assuage the situation that it becomes a self-fulfilling prophecy. During the current covid-19 pandemic, a lot of stress and uncertainty were very common. When will this pandemic end? Will I lose my loved ones? What will be the intensity of the next variant and wave? Are lockdowns going to end? Such questions underlie the stress of uncertainty because answers may be elusive as this is a novel virus and research is still on-going. Even highly acclaimed Virologists and Scientism are admitting to having limited knowledge and information about the "novel" virus.

Personality as a source of stress

As alluded to in the foregoing, personality can be a stress factor in itself. What is personality? Personality is defined as the enduring traits which separate an individual from another. Personality can also be defined as a unique constellation of psychological traits and states. We are as different as we are many and our personality characteristics and dispositions may predispose us to stress in ways we may not conceive. In terms of personality there are also introverts and extroverts. The former are usually reserved and do not like to divulge how they feel and what their concerns are. This thus implies that should something happen, they suffer in silence and have been shown to be prone to stress. Sharing what is troubling and distressing is a good way to relieve pressure and thus the more introverted one is, the more stress can have an impact. Conversely, the extroverted ones are more exuberant and have a propensity and inclination to want to talk about what comes to their minds. In doing so, their personality style would have assuaged the situation and consequently lessened the effects of stress.

CHAPTER 3

Effects Of Stress

Stress has many effects to the body and mind. When the body prepares for "flight" or "fight" response, there are a number of hormones which are released into the bloodstream culminating in heightened alertness and attentiveness. When you encounter situations which elicit a flight or fight response, the mechanism results in blood flow increase, heart palpitations, all this preparing you for the appropriate action. There are so many effects of stress to the individual many of which are negative and result in serious health implications.

Physical effects of stress

Though stress is mainly rooted in negative self-talk and negative evaluation of internal and external factors, which is psychological, it does affect us physically. There is an amazing link between the mind and the body; what happens to the mind affects the body and conversely what happens to the body affects the mind. These two important components work in unison and are inextricable since the whole body is an intricate system.

Headaches

Stress can trigger and intensify tension headaches in the individual experiencing stress. This can lead to further distress as the headache is discomforting in itself and the individual becomes overwhelmed.

Heartburn

Stress increases production to stomach acid and often leading to heartburn. Stress usually makes this condition more pronounced and it is very unsettling.

Insomnia

When one is in a state of heightened vigilance and preparing for a flight or fight response, it is true that sleep disappears. It is only when the real or perceived threat is dealt with that one can be at peace to sleep and the mind is assured that all is now well. Lack of sleep has its own ramifications and effects and thus reduces the overall quality of life of the individual.

Rapid breathing

The muscles which help you breathe tense-up when you experience stress and results in shortness of breath.

Weakened immune system

Long-term stress inevitably leads to a weakened immune system. A weakened immune system leads to vulnerability to various infections and consequently diseases.

Higher risk of heart attacks and high blood pressure

This occurs over a period of time. Since stress is characterized by increased heart rate, high blood pressure to vital organs damages arteries leading to risk of a heart attack. Stress hormones tighten blood vessels leading to narrower arteries and thus blood pressure is increased.

High blood sugar

Stress response communicates with the liver to produce extra sugar or glucose into the bloodstream in order to provide the energy for a flight or fight response. This leads to heightened risk of type 2 diabetes.

Pounding heart

We have invariably seen that when one is stressed the heart rate increases due to stress hormones. This enables blood to reach vital organs and limbs faster to carry out the necessary work. A pounding heart makes one very uncomfortable.

Fertility problems and erectile dysfunction

Stress interferes with the reproductive system in both men and women. This may make child conception a mammoth task. In man, there is a condition called erectile dysfunction. This is characterized by an inability to have and maintain an erection. A stressed brain does not facilitate this process and since the brain plays a crucial role. Stress also causes low sex drive as all faculties are directed towards flight/fight response and other activities are regarded as not urgent. Marital conflicts and infidelity issues can be encountered. Furthermore, stress can result in women missing their periods as a result of fluctuating hormones and disturbing the menstrual cycle. In severe cases, the cycle completely stops.

Stomach ache

Stress has been shown to affect the body's digestive system. This results in stomach aches and related stomach problems.

Tense muscles

Stress makes muscles tense up and chronic stress has been shown to lead to tension-related headaches and backaches. This lowers quality of life and enjoyment.

Psychological Effects Of Stress

Anxiety/Restlessness

Stress increases anxiety and causes confidence and a state of uncertainty about the outcome of events.

Lack of motivation and focus

If one is stressed, it goes without saying that motivation and focus diminish. Concentration becomes difficult and this affects work performance, academic progress and social interactions.

Irritability and anger

We may have encountered a stressed person and usually they are highly irritable and prone to anger. Something that can be considered minor can trigger unmatched anger and vitriol.

Sadness and depression

Persistent feelings of being low and down often characterize a stressed person. This usually occurs if stress has persisted for a long period of time and the individual has concluded that there is no enjoyment in life and thus may withdraw and feel down persistently. Depression is a very serious mental health condition which may require medication (antidepressants).

Behavioral Effects Of Stress

Overeating and undereating

Stress can result in some people either overeating or undereating and those around may not understand what could be happening. Overeating can then result in serious weight gain and obesity and many life-threating health conditions such as heart diseases, blood pressure, and diabetes among others.

Anger outbursts

The stress being experienced may result in anger directed towards people who may not be directly involved or aware of what may be happening. The immediate people may be caught in the cross-fire. The anger is symptomatic of deeper issues the person is experiencing and is not the problem. Conflicts and sociopathic tendencies can result from this behavior.

Drug or substance abuse

Oftentimes, a stressed individual may resort and make recourse to drugs and substances as a way of dealing with stress. This has been shown to lead to even more issues as indulging in drugs and substances abuse may result in an array of health and social problems.

Social withdrawal

Chronic stress may lead to people withdrawing from loved ones, friends and family. Withdrawing however leads to heightened rumination about issues and creates perfect conditions for further mental anguish (angst). Withdrawing is akin to pouring gasoline into the fire. A person with a tendency to withdraw when stressed may even have suicide ideation and needs help urgently!

Lack of exercises

Exercises have been shown to reduce the effects of stress and enhance blood flow thus reinvigorating and refreshing. However, stressed people do not usually take time to exercise thus leading to even more stress.

CHAPTER 4

Symptoms Of Stress

Stress has been recognized as a significant risk factor for diminished physical and mental health in college students and can present several barriers to college persistence (Britt et al., 2017). As such it is important to be alert on the signs and symptoms that commonly appear when one is stressed.

Stress is an inevitable part of life. Stress can affect all parts of your life, including your emotions, behaviors, thinking ability, and physical health. No part of the body is immune. It can take a toll on students' physical health, emotional wellbeing, and academic success unless they learn to manage it appropriately. Stress is a fact of life. Whether students attend college online or in-person, they will most likely face new stressors during their time at school. The majority of adult college students find challenges to balance school with jobs, family, and personal responsibilities as such, students are very likely to experience some or many stressors which may test their ability to cope and adapt to a new environment, balancing a heavy work load, making new friends, becoming more independent and dealing with myriad of other issues.

Fink (2009) defines stress as the emotional and physical strain caused by our response to pressure from the outside world. Put simply, stress is a feeling of being under abnormal pressure, whether from an increased workload, an argument with a classmate or family member, or financial worries.

Everyone experiences stress at some point in life. While it can manifest differently for each individual, it is noted that everyone feels stress at some point in their lives, regardless of age, gender, or circumstance (Currie et al,

2016). In higher education a certain amount of stress is an inevitable and useful part of studying. It assists students to work harder, be focused and return to study rather than doing other things. However, just as everyone is stressed by different things, everyone experiences its effects in different ways.

Stress is unavoidable but it is also manageable at the same time. Today's demands and pressures guarantee that all human beings will experience stress. Changes in our lives such as going to college, getting married, changing jobs, or illnesses are frequent sources of stress. Moving away from home to attend college, for example, creates personal-development opportunities new challenges, friends, and living arrangements however adjusting to these new living arrangements may bring stress in one way or the other. When we do not successfully make these adjustments or changes, we often times find ourselves experiencing a number of unpleasant side effects or signs and symptoms.

When people are exposed to stressors or stimuli that provoke stress, they experience an array of physical, emotional, behavioral, and cognitive reactions. As such, two students might experience stress in very different ways.

How do you know when you are stressed?

When you have too much stress in your life, it can start to manifest itself in external ways. The first step to controlling stress is to know the symptoms of stress. Stress responses have some common signs and symptoms one can look out for. These signs and symptoms are all indications of a level of stress that is not healthy. Below is a list of some of the more common signs and symptoms related to inappropriate levels of stress. They have been categorized as being physical, emotional, cognitive and behavioral (Cohen, 2017). Table 4.1 shows a list of some of the common signs and symptoms of stress that fall under each of the four categories. Individuals can experience symptoms from one or all categories. When you experience these symptoms, you might not feel the motivation you once had to do your best on academic tasks such as preparing for tests or completing assignments. Certain signs of stress can be confused with other ailments, so it is always good to be sure to understand how it affects you so you can correctly identify when you are experiencing stress.

Stress symptoms can be very vague and may be the same as those caused by medical conditions. So, it is important to discuss them with your doctor before embarking on some sort of plan to reduce your level of stress. A medical checkup should first be completed since many of the signs and symptoms identified below could be related to a physical condition.

The following sections briefly detail the categories of stress symptoms.

Physical symptoms of stress

Stress is a normal response to challenging or new situations. This natural reaction has certain physical effects on the body to allow you to better handle the challenges. You can look out for physical signs of stress such as increased heart rate and blood circulation. High levels of stress could lead to physical symptoms that could have a negative effect on student performance. How stress affects the body varies from person to person, but the common physical effects of stress are: frequent headaches, trembling of lips, nervous habits, e.g., fidgeting, rapid or mumbled speech. Refer to Table 4.1 for more physical symptoms.

Emotional/ Psychological stress

Emotional stress involves the experience of negative effects, such as anxiety, in the context of a physiological stress response that includes cardiovascular and hormonal changes. The causes of emotional distress vary widely, and they usually involve a combination of factors. For some people, distress is due to a traumatic experience or event, such as a death in the family. It can also result from a wide range of underlying mental health conditions. The symptoms of emotional distress are sometimes severe and may develop into a mental health disorder. Some symptoms of emotional distress include feeling overwhelmed, helpless, or hopeless, feeling guilty without a clear cause, spending a lot of time worrying, having difficulty thinking or remembering sleeping too much or too little, relying more heavily on mood-altering substances, such as alcohol, isolating from people or activities, experiencing unusual anger or irritability. These symptoms may vary depending on the presence of any underlying mental health disorders. For example, in a person with borderline personality disorder, emotional distress may cause both angry outbursts and intense feelings of loneliness.

Cognitive/Mental Symptoms of Stress

Cognitive stress refers to any kind of stress that affects a person's brain or mind. It is a mental block, a barrier that makes it harder for you to get to where you want to go.

Social/Behavioral symptoms

Behavioral symptoms of stress are persistent or repetitive behaviors that are unusual, disruptive, inappropriate, or cause problems. Some people in stressful times tend to seek out others to be with. Other people withdraw under stress. Also, the quality of relationships can change when a person is under stress.

Spiritual distress

Spiritual pain or distress happens if you have questions and become upset about your belief and value systems. It occurs when a person is unable to find sources of meaning, hope, love, peace, comfort, strength, or connection in life. This may happen when something happens in our life that conflict with our beliefs about ourselves and how we are in the world. It's natural for individuals who have been diagnosed with a terminal illness or who are experiencing great physical or emotional pain to question their beliefs. Spiritual distress can be experienced differently by different people. The signs and symptoms of spiritual distress include:

Feelings of anger or hopelessness
Feelings of depression and anxiety

Difficulty sleeping

Feeling abandoned by God

Questioning the meaning of life or suffering

Questioning beliefs or sudden doubt in spiritual or religious beliefs

Asking why this situation occurred

Seeking spiritual help or guidance

Table 4.1: Signs and Symptoms of stress among students

Physical Symptoms	Emotional/Psychological Symptoms	Cognitive/mental Symptoms	Social Behavioral Symptoms
Irregular bowel movements Involuntary twitching or shaking Irregular or missed periods Getting sick more often than normal Reduced libido Tension headaches Stomachaches Nausea Muscle aches Trouble sleeping Heartburn or indigestion Fatigue Flushed skin Clenched teeth Unusual changes in weight Indigestion High blood pressure Ulcers Heart palpitations Back or joint pain, inadequate oxygen supply, hypoglycemia I (low blood sugar), hormonal and/or biochemical imbalances,	Less than normal patience Feelings of sadness and/or depression Feelings of being overwhelmed Restlessness Reduced or eliminated desire for activities once enjoyed or regularly done Irritability Sense of isolation Trouble coping with life's issues More frequent or extreme pessimistic attitude Fear anxiety, tension, anger, irritation, Hopelessness Helplessness Impatience Depression Nervousness Guilt	Impaired concentration Trouble with remembering things, such as homework assignments or deadlines Impaired speech (mumbling or stuttering) Repetitive or unwanted thoughts Chronic worrying Anxious thoughts or feelings Reduced or impaired judgment Irrational thoughts - "I can't do anything right", "I'm a loser", etc.	Withdrawing from others, Increased irritation with others Change in eating habits Change in sleeping habits New or increased use of drugs, tobacco or drugs Nail biting Pacing Abnormal failure or delay to complete everyday responsibilities Significant change in school or work performance Unusual desire for social isolation Frequent lying Trouble getting along with peers, such as co-workers, classmates or teacher. Change in appetite Sleep disturbance Forgetfulness Angry outbursts Aggression Decline in productivity Social withdrawal Change in sexual interest Increased use of caffeine, tobacco, alcohol, or drugs Indecisiveness Loss of concentration

There is a fairly good possibility that you are experiencing some degree of stress in your life right now, perhaps maybe this very minute. Identify any signs or symptoms that might be occurring regularly in your life, and then determine if the stressor(s) responsible for the side effects is something you may want to deal with.

Given that stress has been linked as a co-factor in 95% or all disease processes, a keystone of holistic, alternative health and healing is learning how to effectively manage stress. This learning process begins with recognizing or identifying the specific types of stress affecting you and how these stressors are showing up or manifesting as symptoms in your life.

CHAPTER 5

Theoretical Framework On Stress Management

There are many theories that have been developed in support of stress management, how it is applied and it's relation to health issues. According to Rice (1999), a theory provides an organized coherent picture of some part of nature or some aspect of human behavior. Moreover, a theory helps to explain and understand the phenomena studied to extend knowledge and to get a greater understanding of the subject. A theory provides a framework in which to organize ideas and experiences: it provides compartments into which knowledge and observations can be fitted and shows relationships between separate pieces of information (Jooste 2008). A theoretical framework must strengthen the subject under study by connecting the researcher to existing knowledge. Transactional Theory will be used in this book.

Transactional Theory

Transactional Stress Model was proposed by Lazarus and Folkman in patients with psychosomatic health conditions (Obbarius et, al. 2021). This theory was proposed in 1966 by Lazarus and is about interactions that takes place between an individual and their environment. The theory focuses on assessments to evaluate damages, threats and challenges that is in an individual. There are external forces which include thoughts, feelings, behaviour and emotions which affect a person in his life. Life events and everyday affairs affect emotions in a person.

The Transactional Theory of Stress and Coping (TTSC) was developed by Dr. Richard Lazarus and Dr. Susan Folkman in 1966 and their framework illustrates how major life events affect human emotions (Janse 2021). The theory focuses on how to deal with stress and coping with it. Change is stressful, and in events, such as divorces, relocation, loss of loved ones or job, etc, an adjustment or reaction is required.

Why Transactional Theory is relevant

Transactional theory is more efficient with environment and individual aspects, more efficient as they share same social system and it is efficient and reliable as adding communicated message also depends on the medium used. It emphasises each individual's role in interpreting what the situation means to them from their perspective rather from someone else's point of view. Stress affect people as individuals not groups so in addressing it needs one to be addressed alone. It allows more variability in the human stress response and helps explain why different individuals respond in different ways to same stressors.

The strengths of this theory is that it focuses on psychological determinants of the stress response over which an individual do not have control and it concentrates on the personal nature and individual's response. Again this theory emphasises an individual's role in interpreting and evaluation on what that situation means to them from their perspective rather from someone else and this enables more variability in the human stress response and helps explain why different individuals respond in different ways to the same stressor. Transactional theory is a dynamic theory that allows that stressors and the circumstances under which they occur can change over time which leads to flexibility.

It considers cognitive approaches.

It caters for individual differences.

It identifies alternative methods for dealing with stress.

The influence of Lazarus and Folkman's (1984) transactional theory of stress and coping is remarkable and remains the cornerstone of psychological stress and coping research across multiple fields (Biggs, Brough and Drummond 2017).

It caters for individual differences - people cope differently and it identifies alternative methods for managing psychological responses of stressors.

The use of transactional models of stress represents a real progress in that it permits to better explain and predict the variety of responses that people show when encountering discrimination and prejudice, as well as the effect of discrimination and prejudice on self-esteem and other adjustment related variables (Major et al., 2003a). Transactional theory offers a unique perspective on work stress from traditional approaches and it has more to do with how best it should be applied to a work setting and one's environment.

Transactional theory has basis for communication because people are viewed as dynamic communicators rather than simple senders or receivers of information, some experiences overlap in order to build shared meaning and messages are interdependent. This theory has a number of elements and processes which are encoding and decoding processes, the communicator, the message and the channel. These help one to communicate and pass the message across when he or she is stressed and this helps the person to get help from family members, friends or counsellors.

Transactional Model of Stress and Coping

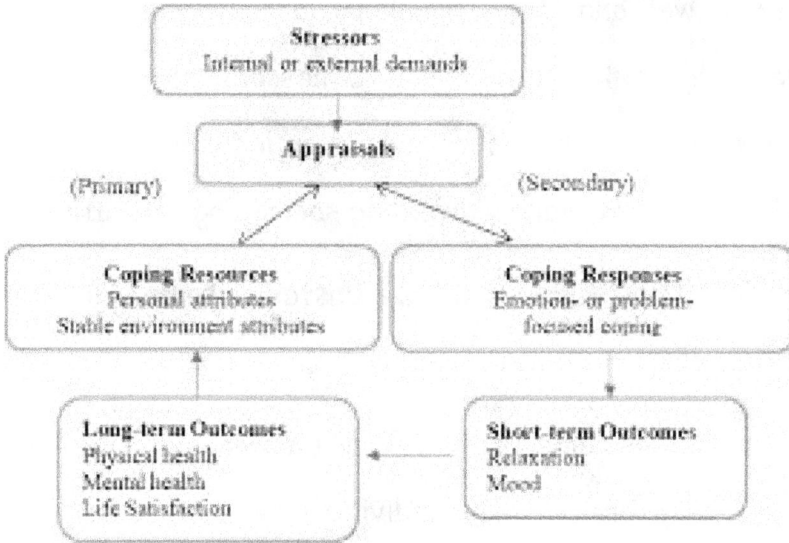

Figure 5.1: Transactional Model of Stress and Coping
(Lazarus & Folkman 1984)

Stressors

Stressors are the physical and psychological demands that initiate the stress response within individuals (Pandey, Quick, Rossi, Nelson, & Martin, 2010). This is what triggers stress in an individual and it includes an employer who is too demanding, relationship that is not going on well and family breakups. Stressors can be from internal or external demands. Stressors can be internal or external and their outcomes in an individual will be low self-esteem, unfriendly, avoiding socializing with others.

Marriages and families will be unstable, some will break, and the children will suffer.

Outcomes in organizations include low productivity, relationship breaking up, individual health affected and death.

Demands exceed the personal and social resources the individual is able to mobilise.

Appraisal

This is an individual's evaluation of what is happening in his/her life and the efforts, action taken to manage the demands of life. Progress in life, results, social life, interaction, work production, ability to cope with work related issues, relating with own family, and health.

Primary Appraisals

Primary appraisal is when an individual examines the relevance of the situation, the degree in which it interacts with personal beliefs, values and goals. Appraisal leads to harm, loss, threat and challenge.

Harm/loss - that has occurred so far.

Threats - potential future harm.

Challenges - How can we learn/gain confidence from this experience?

Primary appraising refers to the process in which an individual examines the relevance of a situation, the degree to which it interacts with personal beliefs, values, goals, and commitments, and potential outcomes if situational investment occurs (Lazarus, 2012).

Secondary Appraisal

Secondary appraising occurs when relationships between person and environment have meaning (Lazarus, 2012). In secondary appraisal, the individual identifies what options are available for handling the situation because he/she is expected to participate in the process of handling the problem at hand. Smith and Lazarus (1993) added that secondary appraising consists of accountability, problem focused coping potential, emotion focused coping potential, and future expectancy.

Secondary appraisal involves the individual evaluating the pros and cons of their different coping strategies. Primary appraisal involves an appraisal of the outside world and secondary appraisal involves an appraisal of the individual themselves. The primary and secondary appraisals determine whether the individual shows a stress response or not.

Lazarus argues that appraising to emphasise active construction of meaning, subject to change as situations are re-evaluated and new experiences, information and beliefs are applied to the constructed meaning. Individual will then engage in secondary appraisal to work out how best we can change undesirable conditions. Evaluate internal and external coping options as well as more specifically resources to create more positive environment internal options - will power and inner strength.

External - peers, professional health

Coping Resources

These are elements that are available to support a person in the stressful situation. When one is stressed there must be coping resources which include personal attributes. These help a person to reduce stress in his body because he has to make an effort to make sure that he is participating in the problem that is at hand. Stable environment entails to the surroundings where the person will be staying and this contributes a lot to the healing. The environment where the person is staying must be welcoming; it is a therapy for the stressed person. As a remedy a stressed person can be moved to another place where the environment is welcoming and conducive.

Long term outcomes

These are results that take place if one is stressed. In transaction theory the long term outcomes include; Physical health, mental health and life satisfaction. It is very important that one copes to stress before long term outcomes affect him/her. These long term outcomes are not good because they affect one's body - health wise and sometimes mental health will be difficult to reverse.

Short term outcomes

Short term outcomes involve one resting and relaxing so that the body rests and be able to cope up with stress. Being in a good mood helps one to cope up with stress. It is good that one be in a good moral most of the time to help reduce stress as per transactional theory.

CHAPTER 6

The Role Of Professional Counsellors In Stress Management

Introduction

Stress has been shown to be very pervasive, a real challenge and a threat to modern society. At basic level, stress is necessary but chronic stress is doubly debilitating. As part of a multidisciplinary team, professional counsellors play a crucial and cardinal role in ameliorating the impact of stress to avoid escalation into serious mental and physical health. Professional Counsellors provide the much needed psychotherapy and counselling services to those in need. They also provide a referral pathway to other mental health service providers after assessment to determine underlying issues which may require psychiatric evaluation and services. This translated into a holistic service that recognizes that some issues presenting have underlying causative reasons which can be explored during therapy sessions.

What is counselling

Counselling is a process of providing professional assistance and guidance for personal and psychological challenges. The counsellor and client set aside time to talk about and explore possible solutions and challenges to presenting challenges. The Counsellor does not tell the client what to do, but instead creates an environment that is conducive, safe and confidential enough for the client to explore challenges and brainstorm about possible solutions., The latter is underwritten by what is called therapeutic alliance, the relationship and ties which lead to insight about the issues and solutions.

What does the Counsellor do?

- ❖ Help the client explore feelings, thoughts and experiences

- ❖ Assist the client to see issues more objectively

- ❖ Clarify issues and generate options from a list of possibilities

- ❖ Make own decision from available choices and not be too dependent on the Counsellor

In addition, the counsellor offers;

1. **Reassurance**-This gives the client confidence in the counsellor and the possibility of presenting challenges being jointly addressed and resolved.

2. **Communication**-Is at the heart of the relationship and resolution of challenges. The Counsellor is an active listener, empathic understanding, good eye contact, nodding, rephrasing, summarizing among others.

3. **Release of emotional tension**-Also called "catharsis" is an important part of therapy which results in better functioning emotionally.

4. **Clarified thinking**-Different activities and processes in the counselling engagement result in clear thinking after exploring different options.

5. **Reorientation**-The client's initial worldview is adjusted as a result of brainstorming and sometimes realistic appraisal of issues.

What are the benefits of counselling?

* Improved communication and interpersonal skills
* Greater self-acceptance and self-esteem
* Ability to change self-defeating behaviors/habits
* Better expression and management of emotions, including anger

- ❖ Relief from depression, anxiety or other mental health conditions
- ❖ Increased confidence and decision-making skills
- ❖ Ability to manage stress effectively
- ❖ Improved problem-solving and conflict resolution abilities
- ❖ Greater sense of self and purpose
- ❖ Recognition of distorted thinking

Common myths about counselling

- ❖ **If I need help, something is wrong with me. I must be broken or abnormal.**
  Just like with physical illness, mental illness and addiction are medical problems. You wouldn't say that someone who has cancer or the flu is broken.
- ❖ **If I come in for an appointment, you will send me to the hospital**

Students are often concerned that if they disclose that they are contemplating suicide, they will be hospitalized or asked to take time off. While the College's highest priority is the health and safety of our students, we understand that many students experience suicidal thoughts without ever acting on them. We work with students to determine what will best address their needs, which often means jointly creating a plan to ensure their safety.

❖ **They will put me on pills that will put me in a fog, and I will never be able to stop taking them** As with physical illnesses, some mental health disorders will require short- or long-term medication regimens. It can be an important part of treatment, but it should never make you feel like you're not yourself or in control.

- **If I just try harder, I won't need treatment**

  Mental health and substance abuse treatment is for people who have an illness that deserves treatment, just as much as any other illness. It can't be cured by trying harder or ignoring the problem.

- **Therapy is just a lot of talking; I can get the help I need from my friends**

  While a strong support system of friends and family is very important, there are things that we can help you with that your loved ones might not be able to. Our training and experience helps us know all the tricky ways that your mental illness can trip you up and how to overcome your hurdles.

- **If I get treatment, I will have to keep going forever**

  Our goal is always to get you back into your "normal" functioning state as quickly as possible.

While some people may need long-term treatment, many individuals just need a few weeks or months to deal with their problem.

❖ **The counsellor will tell me what my problems are and how to fix them**

The purpose of counselling is not to tell the individual what to do. There is no one solution-fits-all. Every person and life situation is unique and needs to be understood. The counselling relationship helps you gain useful insight and understanding of yourself and your situation. This helps you make your own decisions on what the best course of action is for you.

❖ **Once I start counselling I will be in it forever**

The length of counselling depends on the client's goals, motivation, and the severity of the problems. Most counselling is short-term, generally lasting between eight and 15 sessions. Good counsellors are invested in helping you meet your goals so you can successfully operate independent of counselling. Counselling is a process marked not by time but by the quality and outcome of the sessions.

* **Seeking counselling is a sign of weakness**

Asking for help is often seen as a sign of weakness, or that you should be able to fix your problems on your own. This is not true. Admitting you need help can be the hardest barrier to overcome. It takes courage to admit you need help. It requires insight to proactively and responsibly deal with issues before it negatively impacts your physical and emotional well-being and relationships inside or outside the classroom.

* **Counselling is only for severe problems**

Problems that start out as everyday concerns can build up and, if not dealt with, become worse. Counselling offers you a chance to deal with small or large concerns, such as stress, anxiety, life balance, relationships, love triangles, or rectangles, and discover real and effective strategies that work for you. Many people who attend counselling are bright, skilled, and stable people. If you want to be listened to and would like greater awareness, growth, and fulfilment in any area of your life, you may find counselling helpful.

❖ **A counsellor does not know me and can't help me**
This is one of the reasons why counselling can be successful. Since a counsellor is not a part of your day-to-day life, they can offer you impartial, unbiased insights, and support that will help you speak more openly about your situation and remove fears or anxiety about being judged. Counselling involves a unique relationship where you are encouraged and challenged to find the answers that are right for your life.

❖ **Counsellors don't do anything. They just sit there, write notes, and nod occasionally**

Many stereotypes and depictions of counsellors in television and movies have led to their image that counsellors can read your mind, are detached, or ineffective and unable to provide the support you need. The role of the counsellor is to be active.

Conclusion

Professional counselling is strongly recommended for all those who may be facing challenges in their life. It provides an opportunity to talk about and explore possible solutions to challenges in a safe space. All professional counsellors are mandated by ethics to abide by and subscribe to and be compatible with the principle of confidentiality. Most mental health challenges could have been prevented and stresses managed well had counselling been taken as an option and actively sought. Research suggests that over 70% of issues presented to the General Practitioners are psychosomatic in nature. In other words, there was no obvious physical basis for these but invariably tied to psychological challenges, stresses and mental state and anguish. Optimum health and well-being is a sum total of the; physical, mental, social and spiritual well-being not just the absence of disease or infirmity. There is therefore no health without mental health!

CHAPTER 7

How Stress Affect College Students

While students want to perform well in their studies, in their quest to achieve these goals, they could experience situations and events that cause stress. Stress can be triggered by different life experiences. College students have to deal with pressure from many directions. They are more likely to experience worries about grades, limited time and overwhelming workload, finances, relationships, and other social obligations. These factors are often referred to as stressors. When the extent of the pressure exceeds the capacity of an individual, it becomes stressful. Stress then occurs due to gap between demands of these factors and the ability of individual to deal with them (Topper, 2007). Stress, therefore, becomes a barrier for many students to academic success. Understanding the predictors of stress is important in order to help students adjust to the academic environment and for their overall well-being. The following sections highlight how stress is affecting students in academic institutions in their everyday life.

Time Stress

Time stress occurs when you feel worried about time, and more specifically when you do not have enough time to accomplish all necessary tasks. People often experience this when they fear they can't meet their deadlines or will be late to a meeting or appointment.

As a student, you may feel time stress in several different ways whether you are attending college for the first time or you are a returning student. You may worry about being late to your lectures or if it's an online lecture you may worry about facing network or power challenges. You may also panic about the demands of studies such as trying to meet deadlines for assignments, class presentations, tests, and the pressure to prepare for examinations.

In college, you have to figure out the right balance between work, family, and school. The academic load in college is often larger and involves more complicated work than in high school. Attempting to keep up with that, on top of your job and family responsibilities can add additional time stress to your daily life especially if your family and work obligations are so demanding that you fall behind with your schoolwork. Further, balancing your classes, family responsibilities, work schedule, and social life can be hard due to the increased workload. This could lead to an inability to effectively budget and manage time.

As a student you have to fulfil all these demands from several dimensions in order to meet your own expectations and those of your parents (or immediate relatives) and teachers. Time stress is also exacerbated by the fear of failure which usually constantly causes worry and anxiety among students. Time stress is therefore inevitable in a student's life.

Anticipatory stress

Anticipatory stress occurs as a result of a general sense of uncertainty about what's to come. It may be that as an individual you feel anxious about the future or you can be nervous about a particular upcoming event. Students may feel this kind of stress more frequently as they get nearer to the end of term/semester examinations or graduation where they start thinking about their life after college.

You may feel this kind of stress in both a vague and concrete way during your studies. If you feel anxious about a forthcoming test, assignment, or presentation, you are experiencing a more concrete form of anticipatory stress. If you have a sense of dread or fear of uncertainty about your future in general, that is a vaguer manifestation.

Situational stress

In your college days you also experience situational stress when you are in an upsetting or alarming situation that you cannot control. Unlike time-related and anticipatory stress, this kind of stress happens suddenly and with little if any warning. In fact, you may not have anticipated the situation at all.

For students, this type of stress can arise in a number of different circumstances. It may come from something as minor as forgetting your words during a presentation, or as major as a phone call about a family emergency. This kind of stress can occur during a number of situations, from receiving a poor grade on an assignment, to arguing with a friend, to nearly hitting a car in front of you on the road.

Encounter stress

Encounter stress results when you feel anxious about seeing certain people, either alone or in a group. You may not enjoy spending time with them or have difficulties communicating with them. Whatever the reason, there is something about this person or group that makes you anxious. Encounter stress can also occur if you have spent too much time with others and feel burnt out, even if you like being around them.

Students experience encounter stress in situations ranging from intimidating professors to bully classmates. Further, you might only experience this feeling with a person for a limited amount of time. For example, you might dread seeing your roommate for the first time after an argument, but the stress may disappear after you resolve the issue.

Academic Stress

Stress is frequently recognized as a barrier to academic performance. Academic stress refers to college students' response to school and related challenges, such as academic demands, lecturer expectations, course loads, and grades (Acharya et al., 2018; Musabiq & Karimah, 2020; Reddy et al., 2014). Striving to meet assessment deadlines is a major source of stress for many students. College students can also experience academic stress when they try to manage a great deal of academic responsibility and overload themselves with campus involvement. Reddy et al. (2014) found undergraduate students experience more academic stress than graduate students.

Examination Stress

Luckmizankari (2017) alludes that examination stress is a most significant source of stress among students. Examination stress is multifaceted ranging from pre-examination period, the examination period and post examination period.

The pre-examination phase may put students over a high urge to revise and cover the course syllabus before examinations begin. If a student does not schedule the available time, he/she will not be able to cover the syllabus content on time. This lack of preparedness raises anxiety and stress levels. Stress is further exacerbated by the process of tuition payment verification and clearance in order for students to gain entrance to examination halls. Another significant stressor may be related timetable interval between one examination and another. Examination dates and times may be too packed and this may put too much pressure and anxiety on students if it does not give allowance for a breather.

The stress related to the actual examination period relates to stress felt or experienced by students during examinations. A significant stressor in this period is worry that comes as a result of limited time on examination paper duration. Examination time may be too limited to the extent that a student may not nicely complete or finish writing his/her paper. A student may have difficulty in managing his/her time and this may give rise to anxiety on the student while he/she is still in the examination hall. As a student you may also panic, when you see a question and you cannot answer it, or you do not seem to understand it. Your mind may go blank at this moment and this may cause adrenaline rise and you enter into a temporary panic mode. Also, examination hall procedures like ID card verification, signing in attendance registers, long or inadequate examination instructions on question paper and rigid examinations hall rules can trouble the students during exams. A student's place of residence during examination may also have some impact on student's examination stress. It is likely that students who reside in college halls of residences may be less stressed about arriving to exam rooms on time compared to students who reside out of college residence.

Post examination stress rise when students engage in personal thoughts about examinations. A common practice among college students is reflecting on their past examinations and judging whether they will pass the examinations or not. The thought of failing examinations and fear of repeating or getting lower grades can induce depression and pressures after examinations. Post examination stress can be severe if the past experiences, performances and beliefs of the student are negative. High parental or family expectations are likely to increase anxiety and stress levels of students after examinations.

Workload Stress

Workload can be one of the main causes of stress among students. Academic demands and test anxiety are a common long-term cause of stress for college students. College students can experience negative effects of stress from the pressures of balancing coursework and life. Too much time-consuming assignments and reading leave students with no time to relax or socialise with others especially in situations where students have a lot of assignments to do after a very long day. This may end up frustrating for students and affect their focus and thinking levels to the extent that they become unable to cope up with workload efficiently. Even an academically gifted student may feel considerable stress if he/she experiences many deadlines approaching at the same time. This will have a great effect on the academic performance of the student.

Financial Stress

More often, as a student you worry about where your next meal will come from, whether or not you will be able to stay enrolled in college, or whether or not your laptop will take you through your programme of study and whether you will have enough funds to pay for course material. Financial stress is a significant stressor for students living with limited financial resources. Financial stress has been ranked as one of the top five stressors for college students and has been found to be barrier to degree completion for some students (Britt et al., 2016). Everyday living expenses like the cost of housing, clothing, food, and course materials like printing, photocopying and buying books may cause stress and anxiety on students. Lack of pocket money is another significant financial stressor among students in academic institutions. Hossain et al., (2022) found that tuition fee dues have significant positive association with financial stress. A student who has tuition fee dues feels 1.48 times more stress compared to student who does not have dues. Even those students who are supported by scholarships or loans have the stress of keeping up with the standards of the scholarship and making sure their loans are secure.

Preparing for post-graduation life

The prospect of life after college can be daunting simply because it is unknown and unfamiliar. For even the well-prepared student, the unpredictability of life outside of school can be anxiety-inducing. Your stress may be amplified if it seems like all of your friends and peers already have a post-graduation plan that they seem confident about. You might feel anxious if you don't have an idea of what you want to do.

Relationships

Your relationships with friends, family members, and significant other can change after you start college. School may be a bigger priority than ever before, and as you navigate the challenges associated with that; you may have less energy to give to your loved ones. Feeling like you are not as close to your support system, in addition to dealing with the pressures of school, can create tension in your life.

Romantic relationships may act as stressors for college students. When you and your partner face the stresses of college life, the pressure can feel even greater. Additionally, many students may be in the process of questioning their sexuality and/or gender identity, which can impact dating and relationships.

Social Obligations

College students tend to experience high levels of stress when their social lives and social activities are disrupted. Students are more likely to experience stress due to feeling a sense of loneliness, experiencing a breakup, or losing a family member (Acharya et al., 2018). A death or divorce in the family can be extremely traumatic for college students, especially if they live away from home and cannot afford to take a break from classes. College students rely heavily on friends and family for emotional support. Without social and emotional support, college students tend to feel that they are on their own and their stress levels increase drastically (Jones et al., 2018). Hubbard et al. (2018) found that stress related to social obligations can lead to substance abuse in male and female college students, as well as a high rate of depression in female students.

Stress related to studying in a different country

Existing research indicates that students studying in a different country to that of their birth can experience different stressors, and sometimes more pronounced stressors than those reported by home students. Language adjustment challenges and cultural differences may contribute to significant academic stress on students coming from outside the country of study. These students have to cope with the new language both in and outside lecture rooms. It is easy to socially isolate and withdraw from social activities, class participation and other college extra curricula activities in the first year of study. Stress related to home-sickness may also creep in for a student studying in a different country. This may be due in part to the absence of the student's usual support network, such as friends and family.

CHAPTER 8

Practical Strategies To Reduce The Effects Of Stress

Introduction

The previous chapters highlighted that stress is a common phenomenon and is not a bad thing initially. In addition, stress directs our attention to issues needing action but when it causes long-term health, behavioral, physical and emotional abnormal tendencies, concern is raised. We have seen that chronic stress has been invariably linked to serious health conditions which can be life threatening. It is important to realise that as long as one is willing and committed to change and adopt new perspectives about life, prospects of mitigating stress effects become high. In order to live a healthy and fulfilling life, there is need to be proactive and act upon stress early enough. This chapter is devoted to taking a closer look at the practical strategies which can be adopted to deal with and manage stress, reduce the effects and impact of stress. Remember, the key word is "stress management" not "stress elimination!"

Try to figure out the source of the stress you are experiencing

Admittedly, the stress you are experiencing is not coming from all facets of your life. It could be coming from specific aspects. Is it a presentation which you are dreading? Is it because of impending examinations? Is it short-term rush hour traffic? Once you have isolated the stress source, it becomes easier to zero in on the possible ways to mitigate the stress. If your stress is being caused by a presentation that you fear, why not prepare adequately by reading around, listening to guidelines for presentation, engaging those who have presented before, do rehearsals etcetera. By the same token, examination stress requires a student to prepare and adopt proper study and revision techniques. If traffic is causing you stress, why not use alternative means of transport? Remember stress sources can be both internal and external and the more the former, the higher likelihood that you can control it. Sometimes it is better to accept things we cannot change and brainstorm how we can live in a situation than ruminating about conditions we cannot change.

Manage your time

Oftentimes, stress arises from the inability to manage time. Time management like all other skills requires practice, patience and commitment. There is need to analyse how you are currently managing time and if you realise that you are always missing deadlines, then do something about it! There are various time management strategies which if included can reduce stress. Strategies such as; prioritisation, having a to do list, avoiding procrastination, delegating or outsourcing, avoiding being a perfectionist, decision making among others can be tried.

Take a break from a Stressor

Stress often increases when you constantly get transfixed to a project or activity in which there is little progress. When there is little progress, frustration sets in. However, when you take a short break, it can be a fifteen minute to twenty-minute break, new perspectives about the challenge can emerge. Allow yourself this break and you can then resume a task with renewed impetus and energy.

Try breathing exercises

Shallow and superficial breathing has been shown to deprive the body of the much needed oxygen especially in a tense moment. Practice deep breathing even the very moment a stressful occurrence happens. Breathing exercises can be done as follows:

1. Find a comfortable, quiet place to sit or lie down. Choose a spot where you know you won't be disturbed. If sitting, keep your back straight and your feet flat on the floor. Close your eyes.

2. Place one hand on your belly, just below your ribs. Place the other hand on your chest.

3. Take a regular breath.

4. Now take a slow, deep breath. Breathe in slowly through your nose. Pay attention as your belly swells up under your hand.

5. Holding your breath, pause for a second or two.

6. Slowly breathe out through your mouth. Pay attention as the hand on your belly goes in with the breath.

7. Do this several times until you have a calming rhythm.

8. Now add images to your breathing. As you inhale, imagine that the air you're breathing is spreading relaxation and calmness throughout your body.

9. As you exhale, imagine that your breath is whooshing away stress and tension.

10. Try to deep breathe for 10 minutes or until you feel relaxed and less stressed. Gradually work your way up to 15-20 minutes.

Affirmations/positive self-talk

Constantly ruminating about negative things happening only serves to exacerbate the situation. Negative self-talk feeds the mind with negative energy which can lead to the stress response only strengthening. However, it has been shown that positive affirmations help the body to release chemicals which have a calming effect. Whenever, we have an urge for negative self-talk, counter this with a positive one for example; This traffic jam will never end! I shall be late for work! You can counter this and say; The traffic jam is there but eventually it will clear off, I can even call my boss and alert him/her that I may be delayed. Or Let me listen to my favourite motivational speaker, I will not feel it!

Talk about it!

Talking about what is troubling you is often an underestimated stress busting approach. This technique enables the release of pent-up emotion and leads to a better feeling. Those who have shared something troubling then can relate that afterwards one feels much better. Keeping strong and overwhelming emotions can have long-term health dangers. It is thus recommended that you identify a trusted friend, Pastor, Counsellor to talk to and thoroughly vent out. Most people who have committed suicide tended to keep issues to themselves thereby getting overwhelmed with emotions and perceiving that there are no longer options in life. When you share concerns with somebody objective and detached from the situation, this usually elicits alternative views about the situation. You will realise that there may be several options and solutions to the challenges being experienced. Through sharing, you will also realise that you may not be the only one in dire straits but that others are also experiencing life distresses. In some cases, you will also gather that your situation might even be better than your friend's and thus help you to de-escalate the perception of bad situations.

Practice the art of mindfulness

The efficacy and effectiveness of mindfulness has been underwritten by scientific studies. This practice is very simple and can be done in the comfort of your home, school, office and other quiet place. Once you have identified a quiet place, you then choose a one to five word phrase. Repeat the word over and over several times. Take deep breaths in and out slowly focusing on the process as you do so. Take your mind away from other cares and worries while you do so. It is also helpful to set a timer say for about ten minutes. This practice has been shown to release healing hormones which have a calming effect promoting and enhancing relaxation, healing, health and well-being.

Have sound friendship and relations

Human beings are social in nature and thus we all crave association with friends, relatives and even church mates. Never under-estimate the power of interactions and sound relations! People who have deep and sound relations have been shown to be of better sound mental health than those who invariably spend time alone. Laughing together, sharing food, church songs, family gatherings to celebrate different achievements have a very positive bearing on stress by reducing it. Such social interactions are good like medicine! In fact, isolation has been shown to decrease the immune function thereby predisposing one to illnesses leading to reduced life expectancy. Therefore, having friendships and relations is not a luxury but a necessity for sound mental and emotional health.

Pay attention to your diet

Diet affects every facet of our mental and physical well-being. An old adage rightly says "We are what we eat"! The food we eat is responsible for various functions of the body. One of these functions includes stress regulation. If we eat predominantly fast foods or what others call junk foods, our physical and mental health is affected. People who eat ultra-processed foods are more prone to stress than those who eat a balanced diet. Eating an unbalanced diet will lead to several deficiencies thereby affecting stress and mood regulation for example; magnesium and B vitamins.

Minimise phone use and screen time

Smartphones have become an essential part of our lives. Every day, every minute most are glued to their screens. Educational activities, business ventures, church programmes et cetera are now being undertaken online. Thus, the phone is being used for various undertakings which are crucial in the modern times. Notwithstanding, several studies have linked too much time on the screen and smartphone addiction to serious mental health disorders. Too much time spends on the phone is associated with lowered psychological well-being and increased stress levels in both adults and kids. In addition, too much screen time, especially just before bed, affects sleep quality (bluescreen) and leads to higher stress levels due to inadequate sleep. Furthermore, Facebook, WhatsApp, X, Instagram and others give a false impression that other people are enjoying life and that everything is well through the posts. People post very enticing images about holidays, family, parties and other activities and this can evoke the Fear of Missing Out syndrome (FOMO). When people compare, this then increases stress and depression. Smartphone addiction will require commitment to change as some of the effects are much akin to those experienced by drug addicts. Set time when you are not accessing your phone, put it down and do other alternative activities which you enjoy. You can also use an app to track cell phone and internet usage among other strategies. It is also important to interact with people in the face-to-face world rather than online.

Stop comparing!

There is an old adage which contents that; "*cut your coat according to your cloth*". This saying encourages people to live within their means and not pretend to be whom they are not. If you constantly compare your life with that of others and you may currently do not have the resources, this can lead to frustration and stress! Indeed, a measure of comparing and being motivated by what others are doing to succeed is acceptable.

Forgive and forgive more!

Our lives are characterised by interactions with fellow human beings, friends, colleagues, relatives and community members. It is through interactions with others that we encounter conflicts and inter-personal issues. Research studies have shown that people who harbour grudges, conflicts and historical issues are more prone to stress and depression. On the other hand, those who are inclined to forgive when they are hurt, move on and are less prone to depression and stress. It is thus highly recommended that when we are hurt, we train our minds to forgive and realise that human nature is infallible including ourselves. Have you ever noted that when you forgive somebody, you feel as if a heavy clog has been lifted from your chest? It works like medicine! Therefore, learn to forgive and forgive more and you shall live longer and healthily.

Be wary about those whom you interact with

It has often been said that negativity begets negativity and positivity begets positivity. This is very important when it comes to stress management. If you interact with people or friends who are always complaining and have a negative mental propensity, likely you are also going to adopt the same tendency. Such negative people are prone to stress as their prospects about life and about the future in general are invariably grim. There is also the issue of achievement motivation. People with achievement motivation look at challenges and see the prospect of conquering and achieving targets despite the challenges. Conversely, those with low achievement motivation are aligned to dystopia and content with mediocrity. This makes the latter prone to stress as they compare and deem themselves worthless and underachievers.

Get to know your personality style

We are as different as we are many. How many of us are aware about our personality type and how it impacts on how we deal with stress? It is important to know oneself and to do so well. There are people who put frantic efforts in trying to understand others yet they do not even know themselves. For one to know others better, first know yourself. There are different personality types such as; personality type A, type B, and type C. Where do you belong?

Personality type A

According to Sharma (2021), "Type A" refers to a pattern of behavior and personality associated with high achievement, competitiveness, and impatience, among other characteristics.

In particular, the positive traits of a Type A personality include:

Self-control

Motivation to achieve results

Competitiveness

Multi-tasking skills

Meanwhile, the more difficult traits that come with a Type A personality definition include:

Chronic competitiveness

Impatience

Aggression

Hostility

Sharma (2021) posited that because of tendencies to engage in urgent and achievement-oriented behavior, people with a Type A personality may feel more stressed or develop stress-related disorders.

Other characteristics that make people with a Type A personality likely to experience stress include:

Impatience: People with a Type A personality often feel like they're constantly racing against the clock.

Competitiveness: People with a Type A personality are highly competitive and so might criticize themselves a lot when they fail to "win."

Hostility: People with a Type A personality are easily angered and might see the worst in others, sometimes lacking a compassionate outlook.

Achievement-oriented: People with a Type A personality tend to base their self-worth on external achievement and may have a poor work-life balance because of their constant need to prove themselves.

Effect of Type A personality on stress

On the negative traits, aggression is aligned to emotional expressiveness which means when they are faced with stressful situations, they speak or act out. This emotional expressiveness tends to enable a calming effect. Chronic competitiveness and impatience can also lead to stress especially if the anticipated goal is not achieved. The poor work-life balance which type A people exhibit tends to inevitably heighten stress due to lack of rest and sleep. Due to a tendency to be hostile, stress can be induced by conflicts and fights.

Type B Personality

Sharma (2021) avers that people with a Type A personality are often contrasted to people with a Type B personality, which is associated with the following traits:

    Easygoing attitude

    Low competitiveness

    Low frustration

    Lacking the desire to prove oneself

Effect of stress on Type B Personality

Type B Personality oriented people, because of their outgoing tendency, and low frustration tendency are more likely to manage stress better. They see hope and are generally motivated to enjoy life and social interactions. This leverages them to deal with stress and put into perspective external and internal stressors and challenges.

Type C Personality

According to Johns (2023) Type C personality refers to someone who thrives on being accurate, rational and applying logic to everything they do. Demanding logic over emotion is a natural dominant feature. They do not suffer from hype or drama, in fact, they dislike it because they want facts and data. Defined as detail orientated, logical and prepared, this careful, resourceful and thinking personality is very good in a situation where everything needs to be analyzed before any stands are taken. John (2023) further notes that this is one of the more passive personality traits, preferring cooperation over conflict. It can be hard to get the person to open up and they need to have trust in the relationships they have built before they do, leading to a lot of built up tension when decisions are based on anything but the facts laid out. In a working environment, they are meticulous with the information and the data that they have to hand. You will commonly see Type C personalities in roles within science, medicine and law.

Effect of Type C Personality on stress

Due to the fact that Type C oriented people do not usually open up that easily, they can be more prone to stress and mood disorders due to bottling up emotions. Lack of emotional expressiveness leads to an accumulation of emotions over time. This is further exacerbated by the tendency to isolate and ruminate. Isolation provides the perfect conditions for over thinking thus making them more prone to stress and depression.

Conclusion

When it comes to Type A vs Type B personality, there's no clear "winner." As with all personality types, people who fit either the Type A or Type B or C personality type have both positive traits and flaws they should work on. In fact, personality types are best understood as a spectrum with extreme Type A traits on one end and extreme Type B traits on the other. Most people tend to fall somewhere along the spectrum rather than right at its ends.

References

Acharya, L., Jin, L., & Collins, W. (2018). College life is stressful today. Emerging stressors and depressive symptoms in college students. *Journal of American College Health*, 66(7), 655–664. doi:10.1080/07448481.2018.1451869

Biggs, A., Brough, P., & Drummond, S. (2017). Lazarus and Folkman's psychological stress and coping theory. In C. L. Cooper & J. C. Quick (Eds.). The handbook of stress and health: A guide to research and practice. 351–364. Wiley Blackwell. https://doi.org/10.1002/9781118993811.ch21

Britt, S. L., Ammerman, D. A., Barrett, S. F., & Jones, S. (2017). Student loans, financial stress, and college student retention. *Journal of Student Financial Aid*, 47(1), 25-37. Retrieved from https://ir.library.louisville.edu/jsfa/vol47/iss1/3/

Cohen, M. (2017). Surviving stress and anxiety in college & beyond. Retrieved from Learn   Psychology :

http://www.learnpsychology.org/student-stress-anxiety-guide/

Corsica J.A., Bradley L.E. (2018). Stress Management. In: Kreutzer J.S., DeLuca J., Caplan B. (eds) Encyclopedia of Clinical Neuropsychology. Springer, Cham. https://doi.org/10.1007/978-3-319-57111-9_429

Currie C, Molcho M, Boyce W, Holstein B, Torsheim T, Richter M. (2016). Researching health, inequalities in adolescents: The development of the Health Behaviour in School-Aged Children (HBSC) Family Affluence Scale. *Social Science & Medicine.* 66(6), 1429 – 1436.

Dangi R. R, & George M. (2020). Psychological Perception of Students During COVID-19 Outbreak in India Psychological Perception of Students During COVID-19 Outbreak in India. High Technol Lett. 26(6), 142–78. Available from: https://www.researchgate.net/publication/342094992_P

sychological_Perception_of_Students_During_COVID-19_Outbreak_in_India

Eisenberg, D., Gollust, S. E., Golberstein, E., & Hefner, J. L. (2007). Prevalence and correlates of depression, anxiety, and suicidality among university students. The American Journal of Orthopsychiatry, 774, 534–542.

Fink, G. (2009). Stress: Definition and history. In: Encyclopedia of Neuroscience [Internet]. .549–55.Available from: https://www.researchgate.net/publication/285784528_

Goyal, P., Chakrawal, A. K., & Banerjee, R. (2021) Causes of Stress among Students in Higher Educational Institutions in India. Journal of International Cooperation and Development. 4 (1), (48-59). DOI: https://doi.org/10.36941/jicd- 2021-0003

Hossain, M.D., Mahfuz, T., Latif, S., & Hossain, M.E., (2022). Determinants of financial stress among university students and its impact on their performance. Journal of Applied Research in Higher Education. Vol. ahead-of-print.

Hubbard, K., Reohr, P., Tolcher, L., & Downs, A. (2018). Stress, mental health symptoms, and help-seeking in college students. *Psi Chi Journal of Psychological Research*, 23(4), 293-305. https://doiorg.lynx.lib.usm.edu/10.24839/2325-7342.JN23,4.293.

Janse, B. (2021). *Transaction Theory of Stress and Coping (TTSC)*. Retrieved on 21 May 2023 from Toolshero: https://www.toolshero.com/psychology/transactional-theory-of-stress-and-coping/

Jones, P. J., Park, S. Y., & Lefevor, G. T. (2018). Contemporary college student anxiety: The role of academic distress, financial stress, and support. *Journal of College Counselling*, 21(3), 252–264. doi:10.1002/jocc.12107.

Jooste, K. (2008). Leadership in Health Services Management. Cape Town: Juta.

Lazarus, R. S. (2012). Evolution of a model of stress, coping, and discrete emotions. In V. Hill-Rice (Ed.), Handbook of stress, coping, and health (2nd ed.). Thousand Oaks, CA: SAGE Publications.

Lazarus, R. S. (1966). *Psychological stress and the coping process.* New York: McGraw Hill.

Luckmizankari, P. (2017). Factors Affecting on Examination Stress among Undergraduates: An Investigation from Eastern University. *IRE 1700063 Iconic Research and Engineering Journals.* 1(4), 9-15. ISSN: 2456-8880

Musabiq, S. A., & Karimah, I. (2020). Description of stress and its impact on college student. *College Student Journal,* 54(2), 199-205. https://search ebscohostcom.lynx.lib.usm.edu/144419165&site=ehost-live.

Nevid. J. S. (2012). Essentials of psychology: Concepts and applications. 3rd edition. Wadsworth Cengage Learning: Australia.

(2013) Stress. In: Gebhart G.F., Schmidt R.F. (eds) Encyclopedia of Pain. Springer, Berlin, Heidelberg. https://doi.org/10.1007/978-3-642-28753-4_202153

Major B., McCoy S. K., Kaiser C. R., Quinton W. J. (2003a). "Prejudice and self-esteem: a transactional model," in *European Review of Social Psychology,* Vol. 14, eds Strobe W., Hewstone M. (London: Psychology Press;), 77–104

Obbarius N, Fischer F, Liegl G, Obbarius A, Rose M. (2021). A Modified Version of the Transactional Stress Concept According to Lazarus and Folkman Was Confirmed in a Psychosomatic Inpatient Sample. Front Psychol. 2021 Mar 5;12:584333. doi: 10.3389/fpsyg.2021.584333. PMID: 33746820; PMCID: PMC7973375.

Pandey, A., Quick, J. C., Rossi, A. M., Nelson, D. L., & Martin, W. (2011). Stress and the workplace: 10 years of science, 1997-2007. In R. J. Contrada & A. Baum (Eds.), *The handbook of stress science: Biology, psychology, and health* (137–149). New York: Springer Publishing Company.

Pastorino E. and Doyle-Portillo S. (2012). What is psychology? 3rd ed. Wadsworth Cengage Learning: Australia.

Reddy, S., Reddy, P., & Reddy, D. (2014). A comparative study on sources of stress and coping styles between graduation and post-graduation students. *Indian Journal*

of Health & Wellbeing, 5(8), 942-947. https://search
ebscohostcom.lynx.lib.usm.edu/login.aspx?direct=true&db
=aph&AN=98997627&site=ehost-live.

Ribeiro, Í. J. S., Pereira, R., Freire, I. V., de Oliveira, B. G.,
Casotti, C. A., & Boery, E. N.   (2017). Stress and quality
of life among university students: A systematic literature
review. Health Professions Education. Retrieved from
http://www.sciencedirect.com/science/article/pii/S2452
301117300305 [Google Scholar]

Rosch, P. J. (2021). Reminiscences of Hans Selye, and the
Birth of "Stress". The American Institute of Stress.

Selye, H. (1974). *Stress without distress.* New York, NY:
Lippincott.

Shahsavarani, A. M, Abadi, E. A. M and Kalkhoran, M. H.
(2015). Stress: Facts and Theories through Literature
Review. *International Journal of Medical Reviews, 2 (2),
230-241*

Smith, C. A and Lazarus, R. S. (1993). Appraisal
components, core relational themes, and the emotions.
Cognition and emotion. 7(3/4), 233-269.

Topper, E. F. (2007). Stress in the library workplace. New Library World. 11/12, 561-564.